گەشتێک بەناو هونەری ئیسلامی دا

Journey through Islamic Art

Na'ima bint Robert & Diana Mayo

mantra

چە ند داستانێکم دەربارەی شارەکانی سەمەرقەند و بەغدا،
و مگۆلیەکانی هند و موورەکان لە ئیسپانیا بیستبوو.

I heard tales about the cities of Samarkand and Baghdad,
About the Moghuls in India and the Moors in Spain.

رایه له ئاوریشمییه کانی مێژووم له ناو له پی ده ستم کۆکردەوه و،
ئاوەزم جبه یه کی فرۆکی لێ چنین:
ئه م جبه یه بوو که سه فه رێکی سه یر
و سه مه ره به ناو هونه ری دنیای ئیسلامی پێ کردم.

I gathered silken threads of history in my hands and,
With them, my mind wove a flying cloak:
A cloak that took me on an amazing voyage
Through the art of the Islamic world.

جبه که م بردمیه شاره کۆنه که ی به غدا،
مه کۆی مزگه وت، حه مامی گشتی،
ریبازی کیٚ به رکیٚ و ره شماٚله کان.

My cloak took me to the old city of Baghdad,
Home to mosques, public baths,
racetracks, and pavilions.

مه‌کۆی قه‌ڵای هه‌ڵه‌ مووتی سه‌حرایی،
ڕازاوه‌ به‌ نه‌خش و نیگاری سه‌ر دیوار
له‌ سه‌ر هه‌ردهوه‌ تا سه‌ر میچ.
گه‌وره‌ترین مزگه‌وت له‌ سه‌رتاسه‌ری دنیا ناوی سامه‌ڕایه‌،
وام زانی بانگی ئه‌م مزگه‌وته‌ هه‌وری ئاسمانی بڕیوه‌
و گه‌یشتۆته‌ من.

Home to fortified desert castles,
Adorned with wall-paintings from floor to ceiling.
The largest mosque in the world called Samarra its home,
I imagined that the call to prayer reached me in the clouds.

جبه که م منی برده لای موسلّمانه کانی ئیسپانیا،
له م شوێنه دا بوو که رۆژهه لّات و رۆژئاوا به یه ك گه یشتن.
سه ردانی زانست وانان، داهێنه ران و ئاسمان پشکنانم کرد،
سنووری زانیاری مرۆڤیان به تاقی ده کرده وه.

My cloak took me to Muslim Spain,
Where the East met the West.
I passed scientists, inventors and court astronomers,
Testing the limits of human knowledge.

لەم شوێنەدا بە سەرسامییەوە بەناو حەوشە رازاوەکانەدا گەرام،
بەقەراغ ئاوەڵدێر و باخچە بۆنخۆشەکاندا تێپەرِ بووم.

There, I wandered through ornamental courtyards,
Past fountains and scented gardens.

میراتی هونەری ئیسلامی
و ئیسپانی ئاوێتەی یەکتر بوون
و کۆشکی ئەل حەمبرا و گەورە
مزگەوتی کۆربۆدایان بەرهەم هێنا.
گومبەز، کاشی و تاقەکان خۆشی
و چێژیان بە چاوەکانم بەخشی.

The artistic heritage of
Islam and Spain
Fused to create the
Al Hambra palace and
the great mosque of
Cordoba.
Domes, mosaics and
archways greeted my
eager eyes.

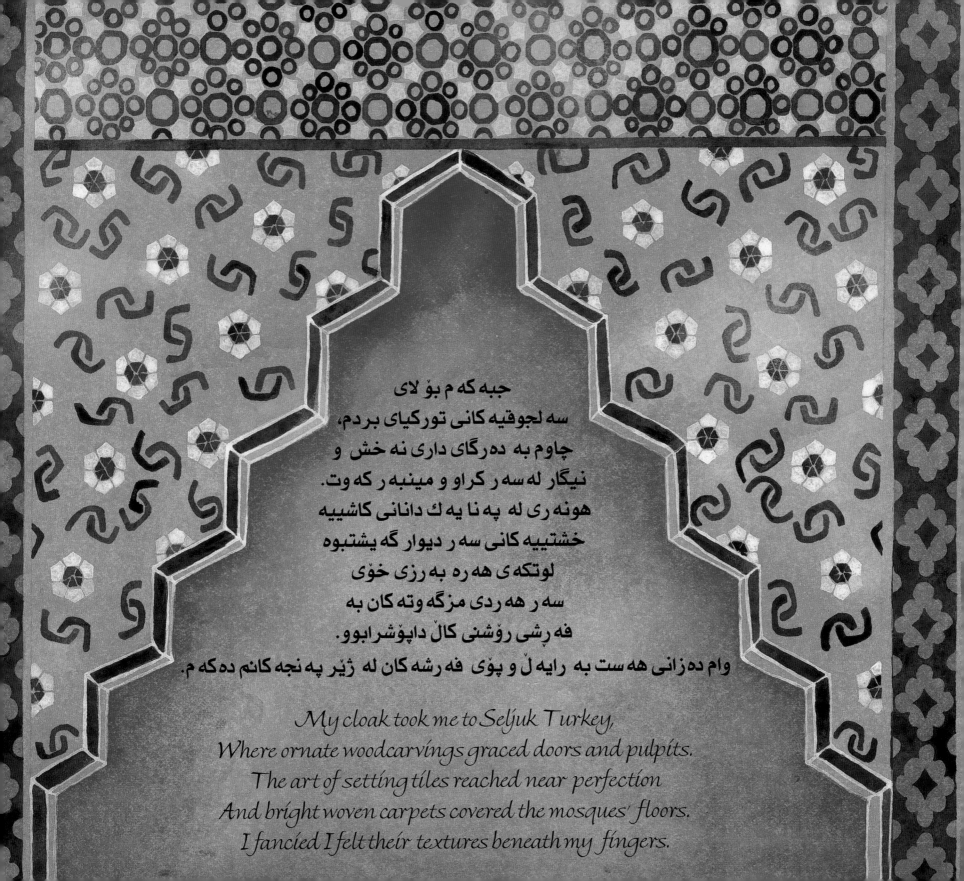

جبه که م بۆ لای
سه لجوقیه کانی تورکیای بردم،
چاوم به ده رگای داری نه خش و
نیگار له سه ر کراو و مینبه ر که وت.
هونه ری له په نا یه ك دانانی کاشییه
خشتییه کانی سه ر دیوار گه یشتبوه
لوتکه ی هه ره به رزی خۆی
سه ر هه ردی مزگه وته کان به
فه رشی رۆشنی کاڵ داپۆشرابوو.
وام ده زانی هه ست به رایه ڵ و پۆی فه رشه کان له ژێر په نجه کانم ده که م.

My cloak took me to Seljuk Turkey,
Where ornate woodcarvings graced doors and pulpits.
The art of setting tiles reached near perfection
And bright woven carpets covered the mosques' floors.
I fancied I felt their textures beneath my fingers.

جبه‌ که‌ م به‌ ره‌ و شاری سه‌ مه‌ رقه‌ ند
و ته‌ یمووری له‌ نگی بردم
کارجوانانی هه‌ موو دنیا له‌ م شاره کۆببوونه‌ وه‌.

My cloak took me to the Samarkand
of Timur 'the Lame'
Where artisans from around the world
were gathered.

به ردتاشه کانی هندستان،
خه‌ت خۆشه کای ولاتی فارس،

Stonemasons from India,
calligraphers from Persia,

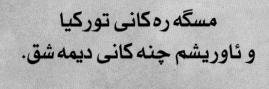

مسگه‌ره‌کانی تورکیا
و ئاوریشم چنه‌کانی دیمه‌شق.

Silversmiths from Turkey and
silk-weavers from Damascus.

تەیموری لەنگ هەمووانی بە دیل گرتبوون بۆ ئەوەی شارەکەی بۆ برازینەنە وە هەرچەندە کۆشکی خۆی خێوەتێک بوو ـ لە راستی دا کە سێکی کۆچەر بوو.

All brought back as captives, to beautify his city,
while his palace was a tent – a nomad to the end.

جبه که م به ناو شه قامه کانی ئاگرا دا گه رِاندمی،
ده نگۆی تاج مه حه ل بازارِه پرِ له جم و جۆلّه کانی ئه م شاره ی پرِکردبوو.

My cloak took me to the streets of Agra,
Where rumours of the Taj Mahal filled buzzing bazaars.

ئه‌م شوێنه‌ له‌ به‌دی هێنانی ئاواتێکی که‌ سێکی
سه‌ره‌مه‌رگه‌وه‌ هاتۆته‌ ئاراوه‌
ئه‌و خامه‌ سپییه‌ی له‌ به‌ر خۆی کردبوو
له‌ به‌ر رۆشنایی خۆرا ده‌ دره‌ وشایه‌وه‌ .

A building born from a deathbed promise,
Its garment of white marble
Shimmered in the light.

المشرق

خۆشنووسراوەكانى ئايەتەكانى قورئان،
كاشييە گوڵدارەكانى سەبكى ئيسلامى
و نيگارە ھەندەسييەكان
لەگەڵ يەك ھەماھەنگ بوون

شاعيران ناويان لێ ناوە 'روخسارى روو لە گزنگ'.
ئارەزووم دەكرد خۆزيا ئەم شوێنە ژيانى گرتبايە خۆ
و ئارامگاى مردووان نەبا.

صباح الفجر

Calligraphic inscriptions from the Qur'aan,
Floral arabesques and geometric designs
all harmonised
And the poets named her 'Dawn's bright face'.
I wished its beauty could grace the living
and not enshroud the dead.

ئەم گەشتە خەونێك و، خولیای مندالێك بوو،
هەر چەندە ئەم شوێنانە بە ڕاستی هەن.
ئارەزوومە جبەکەت بەم داستانە بسووڕێ
و تۆش بۆ ئەم شوێنانە بەڕێ.

This voyage was a dream – a child's fantasy,
Though all its destinations are true.
I hope that your cloak will be spun by this tale
And that you will go there too.

Here are some explanations to help you enjoy the story:

Samarra
In the 9th century, after the foundation of Baghdad, the Caliph (ruler) moved his capital to the splendid city of Samarra. The Great Mosque was once the largest mosque in the Islamic world and rises to a height of 52 meters.

Islamic Spain was established in the 8th century by Muslims from North Africa who were known as Moors. For over three hundred years, Muslims, Christians and Jews lived together in a Golden Age when learning, art and culture flourished.

Seljuk Turkey was one of the eras in Islamic history. The Seljuks were Muslim rulers who took control of Persia and Turkey. Seljuk Turkey became the centre of excellence in weaving, ceramic painting and wood carving.

Born in the 14th century, **Timur 'the Lame'**, also known as Tamerlane, was a fierce and determined Mongol warrior who loved art. Whenever his armies invaded foreign cities, he would take care to protect the artisans and take them back to beautify his city, Samarkand.

The **Taj Mahal** was a monument built by the Mughal Emperor Shah Jahan in 1631 as a tribute to his loving wife Mumtaz Mahal. Legend says that she made him promise to build her a mausoleum more beautiful than any the world had ever seen.

Arabesque is an art form originally from Asia Minor. It was later adapted by Muslim artisans into a highly formalised form of intertwined flowers and plants.

The Qur'aan, the Muslim holy book, was revealed to the Prophet Muhammad (pbuh) by the Angel Gabriel. Its verses are often inscribed in beautiful patterns by calligraphers.

First published in 2005 by Mantra Lingua
Global House, 303 Ballards Lane, London N12 8NP
www.mantralingua.com

A CIP record for this book is available from the British Library.

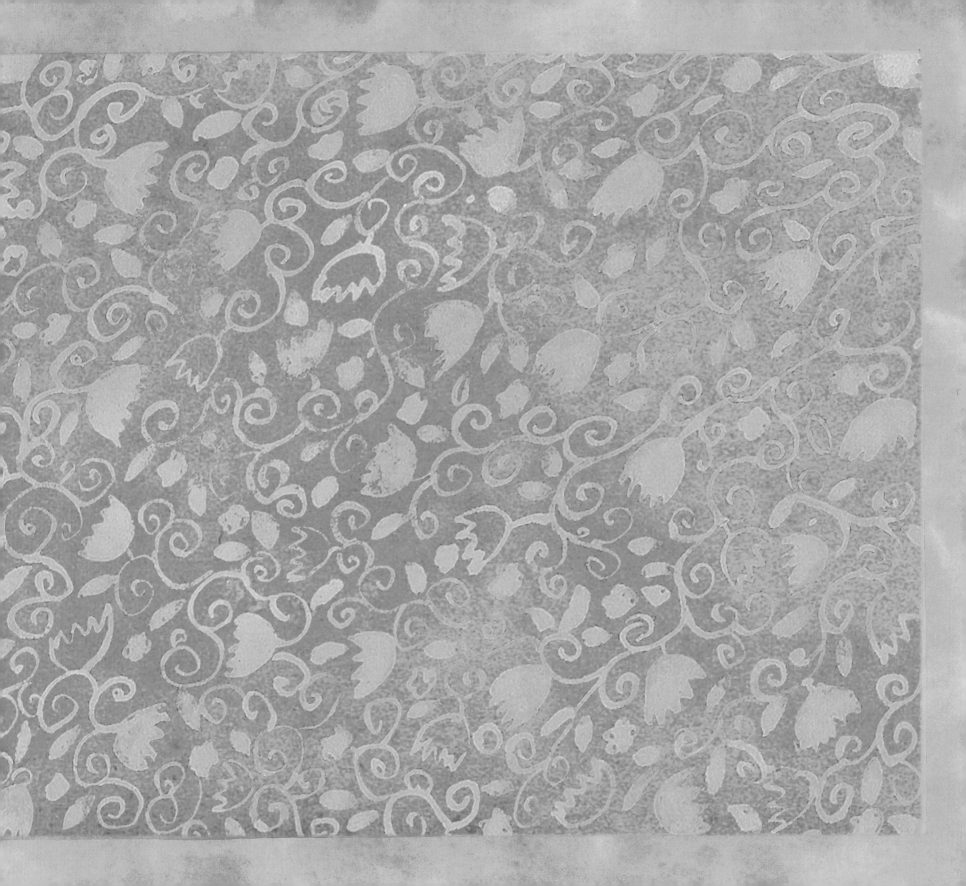

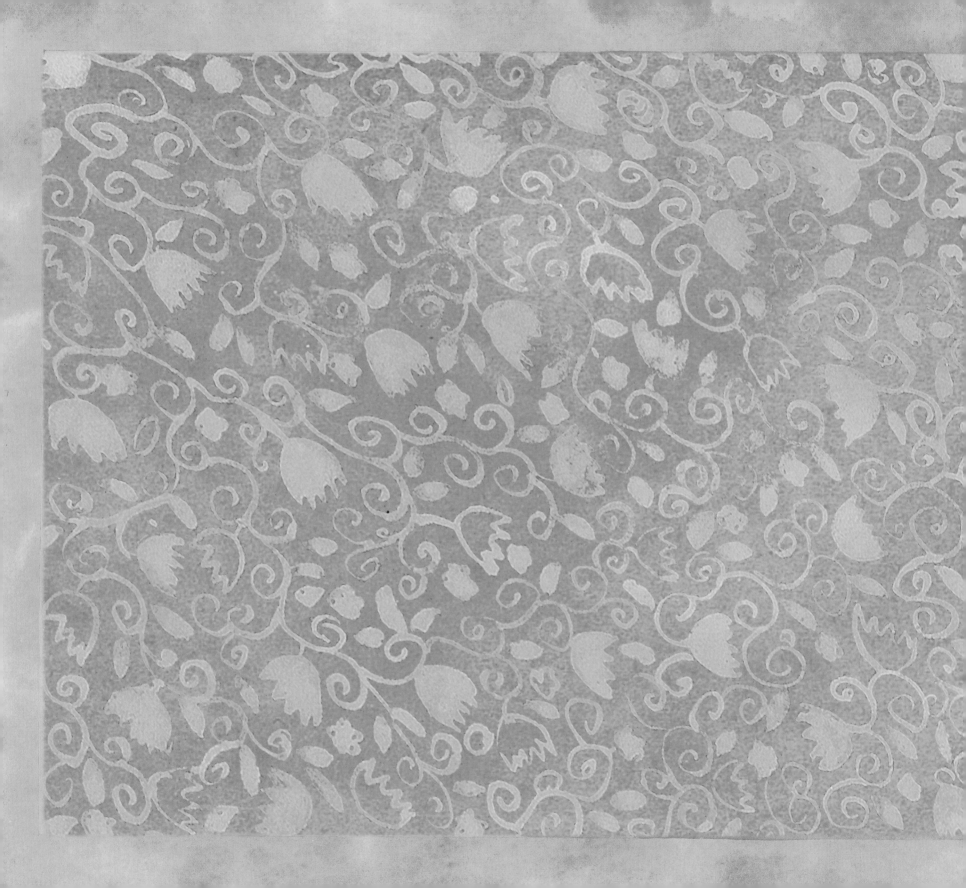